FIT FOR THE GAME
SOCCER

Theo Foley

WARD LOCK

Editor: Heather Thomas
Art Director: Rolando Ugolini

Text set in Univers Medium by Halcyon Type & Design Ltd, Ipswich
Printed and bound in Great Britain by Richard Clay Ltd

**British Library Cataloguing in Publication
Data**

Foley, Theo
  Soccer.
  1. Sports. Physical fitness
  I. Title II. Series
  613.711

ISBN 0-7063-6935-1

Theo Foley

Theo Foley began his footballing career at Home Farm in Dublin, one of the best clubs in Eire. In fact, over 20 players from this club went on to become full internationals.

In 1954 he joined Exeter City in England and made his debut in 1955 aged eighteen. He played over 260 games for Exeter before his transfer to Northampton which had just gained promotion to the Third Division. He went on to play in the Second and First Divisions, and as an international for Eire five times between 1963 and 1967.

In 1967 Theo went to Charlton Athletic as coach, later becoming manager, but left in 1974 to join Gordon Jago at Millwall as coach. After a spell at Queens Park Rangers, coaching such players as Clive Allen, Paul Goddard and Gary Waddock, he went to Millwall with George Graham.

In 1984 he followed George Graham to Arsenal and the years that followed were great years for the club, winning the Littlewoods Cup 2-1 against Liverpool in 1985 and winning the First Division Championship 2-0 against Liverpool on May 26 1988 – a night that Theo will never forget!

In June 1990 he returned to his old club Northampton, but this time as manager.

Acknowledgements

The author would like to thank everybody who helped him on this book, especially David O'Leary.

The publishers would like to thank Northampton Town Football Club for their assistance, Denis Casey, the physiotherapist, and the following players who appeared in the photographs: Phil Chard, Terry Angus, Kevin Wilkin and Paul Wilson.

All the photographs are courtesy of Mark Shearman with the exception of the cover photograph of David O'Leary which was supplied by AllSport and page 6.

CONTENTS

FOREWORD
by David O'Leary

I always used to look forward to my warm-up sessions with Theo Foley at Arsenal before we even started to kick a ball. I am the type of player who likes to be warmed-up before I touch the ball, so Theo's mixture of good humour, exercises and running for about twenty five minutes was ideal for all of us at Arsenal.

We would run for five minutes followed by some stretching exercises and then jog around, gradually increasing the pace. Then we would stop and do some more stretching, going further on each exercise as we were by then well warmed-up. And to finish this warming-up session, we would do some stride-outs racing against each other. We were then ready for George Graham to start the next stage of the training session.

Over those four years at Arsenal with Theo we had hardly a muscle injury between us in training. I am convinced that this was due to Theo's warm-ups, and it proves to me the importance of having a good coach, which Theo undoubtedly was, and warming-up thoroughly before a training session or match.

At whatever level of soccer you play, fitness can help you to play better and to get more enjoyment out of the game. Your own personal level of fitness can help to give you an edge over your opponents and make all the difference between being a good or a mediocre player. I hope that you get some benefits and some fun from doing the exercises and drills in this book.

INTRODUCTION

This book is specifically designed for soccer teams and individual players who train in confined spaces and possess the minimum amount of training equipment. It is aimed at teams who play in local parks, on company grounds, school or college grounds. These teams are normally youth clubs, company teams, pub teams or a group of young men who have got together to form a soccer team. It is also aimed at teams who do their pre-season training in the local parks and season training in a confined space, normally the gymnasium of a local school, in the evenings. All the exercises can also be used by teams who do their season training out-of-doors.

The exercises are mainly isometric. The only equipment needed is as follows: footballs, gymnasium benches and cones. Where this equipment is unavailable or insufficient in number you can improvise with a medicine ball for footballs, chairs for gymnasium benches and kit bags or corner flags for cones. Where floor-level wall bars are required for abdominal exercises and are not available, improvise by turning a gym bench upside-down and use the cross-support strut as a wall bar.

I have targeted teams who do not have a qualified coach or trainer, but where the team manager, club secretary or another volunteer acts as trainer. With this in mind I have made the exercises easy to understand and follow. Different training schedules can be designed by combining different exercises to ensure that the full range of muscles used during a game of soccer are fully exercised.

The fitter you are; the more strength, endurance, speed and flexibility you possess, the better a player you will become. It is no good having the basic skills and techniques and tactical ability if you do not have the physical fitness to back these up. As you become fitter and stronger, your game will improve, and you will have more stamina to keep you going and playing well without tiring in a long match.

CHAPTER ONE

WARM UPS

The value of warm-up sessions before training or on match day is often questioned by many players, but I believe that they are extremely beneficial. The Institute of Cardiology in London states that after a preliminary exercise period, subsequent exercise is performed more efficiently as far as oxygen utilization and cardiovascular work are concerned. Thus a preliminary exercise period will have a positive effect on any subsequent exercise, and this will be of benefit to players.

Muscle fatigue can be delayed by doing preliminary exercises before undertaking maximal muscle work. One of the benefits of warm ups is the opening up of the blood vessels in the muscles that are to be used. Other benefits include:

● A rise in pulse rate which, in turn, increases circulation.

● An increase in body temperature which reduces muscles' viscosity helping to prevent strains and partial tears in the main muscle groups used in football.

● An improvement in the extensibility of muscles enabling them to stretch through their full range.

● An improved transport system to get glycogen (muscle sugar), oxygen and blood to muscles and body cells plus an energy transfer system.

Before taking part in any activity, you should put all the joints involved through a full range of movements. Mobility exercises are therefore an important part of a warming-up routine – merely to jog around for 20 minutes is virtually useless. Match-day warm ups also help to relieve or decrease pre-match tension in players, making them more relaxed mentally and less stiff physically at the start of the game. Regular stretching routines can become an intrinsic part of everyday life, bringing a wide range of benefits:

● Increasing your range of motion.
● Protecting against and preventing muscular injuries.
● Helping to develop general body awareness.
● Reducing muscular tension.
● Promoting good circulation.
● Increasing physical co-ordination.

Ideally before each work-out or training session, you should warmup for about 20-30 minutes, stretching the whole body but focusing specifically on the legs. Here is a general warm-up session for you to follow:
1 Chest flings
2 Arm circling
3 Side stretches
4 Hip rotations
5 Shoulder shrugs
6 Hamstring stretch
7 Groin stretch
8 Adductive stretch
9 Calf stretch
10 Neck rotations
11 Back arches

And don't forget that at the end of every session it is equally important that you 'warm-down'. This will ease out muscles and help prevent muscle stiffness and injury. Light jogging and stretching for 5-10 minutes are an excellent way to do this.

Warm-up exercises

Chest flings *below*
1 Stand upright with your feet shoulder-width apart and elbows bent at shoulder height with fingertips touching.
2 Fling your arms out backwards at shoulder height. Do 10 repetitions.

Arm circling *below*
1 Stand upright with legs shoulder-width apart, and arms outstretched to the sides at shoulder level.
2 Circle your arms clockwise for 10 repetitions, making large circles. Then repeat 10 times in an anti-clockwise direction.

Side stretches *right*

1 Stand upright with your feet shoulder-width apart and knees slightly bent.
2 Raise one bent arm above your head and slide the opposite arm slowly down the side of your leg. Repeat on the other side. Do 10 repetitions on each side.

Hip rotations *below*

1 Stand with your legs apart and lift and bend one knee.
2 Push the bent knee across your body to touch the opposite hip. Repeat 10 times, and then repeat with the other leg.

Shoulder shrugs

1 Stand with your hands on your hips.

2 Shrug your shoulders to rotate them backwards and forwards 10 times.

Hamstring stretch: 1

1 Sit on the ground with your legs as wide as possible and grab your right thigh with both hands.

2 Without bending your knees, slide both hands down your right leg as far as possible. Repeat 10 times, then change legs.

Groin stretch *right*

1 Stand with one leg about one stride in front of the other.
2 Bend your front leg, transferring the weight onto it, and keeping your back leg straight. Repeat 10 times with each leg.

Adductive stretch *below*

1 Standing with legs as far apart as possible, grab your right thigh with both hands.
2 Slide both hands down your leg as far as possible. Repeat 10 times. Change legs.

Calf stretch *below*

1 Stand with one leg one stride in front of the other, bending both knees slightly.
2 Continue bending forwards at the knees, keeping both feet flat on the ground. Repeat 10 times. Change legs.

Back arches *below*

1 Stand in an upright position with knees slightly bent, and place your hands on the back of each thigh.
2 Work both your hands down the backs of your legs without over-straining yourself. Repeat 5 times.

Neck rotations *right*

1 Stand upright and relaxed with arms behind your back.
2 Gently and slowly roll your neck clockwise. Do 10 repetitions and then repeat in an anti-clockwise direction 10 times.

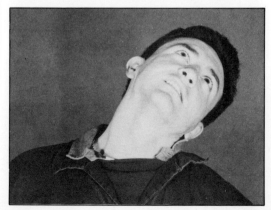

Additional warm-up exercises

Jogging drill

Jogging around the perimeter of a gym or pitch and on the command of the trainer, whilst still jogging, do the following:

1 Touch the ground to the side with fingertips of one hand. Repeat 5 times and do the same with the other hand. This exercise is designed to keep backs supple.

2 Jump to head an imaginary football. **Note:** Goalkeepers should jump with both arms fully extended above the head as if to field a high ball. Repeat 5 times.

3 About turn. Jog 10 yards and stop. Jog 10 yards backwards and stop. Jog 10 yards sidewards and stop. All this emulates what happens during a match. Repeat 5 times.

4 Kick your heels up back, touching the right heel with the right hand and vice versa. Kick an imaginary ball – first with the right foot and then with the left one. Repeat 5 times.

5 Place some benches around the perimeter to hurdle over if you are in a gym. Do 5 circuits.

Passing drill

1 Perform this exercise in pairs. Stand 10 yards apart. Player A has a football and makes a diagonal pass for his partner (B) to sprint to, collect and control.

2 Player B then makes a diagonal pass for his partner to also sprint to, collect and control. Repeat 5 times.

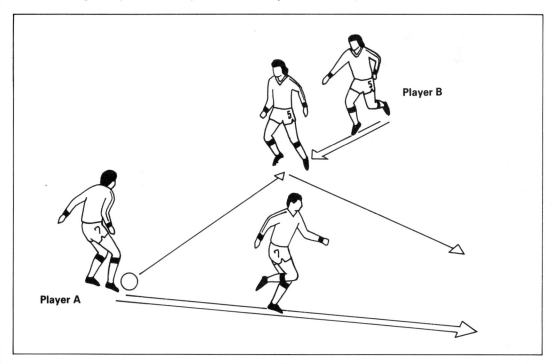

Player B

Player A

Side-stepping drill

Facing sideways to a wall, side-step across the gym to the other side. Repeat 5 times.

Opposite command exercise

1 This exercise is useful in increasing players' ability to concentrate; a vital factor during a game. On the trainer's command players do the opposite to what is asked of them. For example, if commanded to jump in the air, they touch the ground, and vice versa.

2 Place two sets of markers at either side of a column of players. A command for the players to touch the marker on the right means they should sprint to the marker on the left.

3 Players who get it wrong do five press-ups. Between commands players should run on the spot.

Half-squats

1 Stand with your left leg extended in front of you, and your right leg behind you.

2 Now jump rhythmically, changing the legs – right leg to the front, left leg backwards and so forth.

3 Raise your arms to the side. Lower.

4 Raise them above your head and clap hands. Repeat 5 times.

Jumping jacks *below*

1 Stand with feet together. With a rhythmic movement jump with feet astride sideways.
2 Bring your feet back together.
3 Without stopping, raise your arms to shoulder level and then lower back to your thighs.
4 Still jumping, raise your arms above your head and clap your hands. Repeat 5 times.

Knee lifts

1 Jog on the spot, raising your knees.
2 Then run full-out on the spot to knee-high for 10 seconds.
3 Jog on the spot again, then all-out effort running on the spot for 15 seconds.
4 Jog again, and continue in this way increasing the all-out effort running by 5 seconds each time until 30 seconds is reached.

Hopping drill

1 Standing, extend your left leg out sideways, and at the same time extend your right arm up above your head.
2 Hop to extend the right leg out to the side and raise the left arm above your head. Try to establish a hopping rhythm. Repeat the exercise 10 times with each leg.

Soldier drill *below*

1 Standing on the spot, extend your left leg in front of you, foot touching the ground, and raise your right arm in front of you at shoulder height.
2 Now jump, landing with your right leg in front and left arm extended. The movement should be that of a marching soldier.
3 When the forward arm is at shoulder height, roll the arm backwards to touch shoulder blade with finger-tips. Try to obtain a swinging rhythm. Repeat 10 times.

CHAPTER TWO

STAMINA BUILDING

In this chapter I am going to deal with increasing players' level of stamina and their determination. You need stamina and endurance to compete in a game of soccer; more so when the ground becomes muddy and heavy. It is also essential when a cup-tie goes into extra time, and the last ounce of stamina and determination must be extracted from every player to get a good result and get through to the next round.

Some of the exercises described are designed to bring out the competitive instinct in the players during training. Competing is a vital part of soccer and should be used during training sessions, so that on match day, it will be instinctive for the players to compete against their competitors.

Building up general physical stamina can also be achieved by running, swimming, cycling, walking and skipping. You will need to be motivated and must be prepared to work hard to attain the level required to play soccer well. You can work out your own training regime to supplement the training you do with your team. This can be very flexible and can be done at home, in the gym, in your local park or wherever suits you personally. All you need is the right dress and the correct expertise and technique.

Running requires either some local parkland, countryside, roads or a beach where you can train and gradually build up to 40 minutes of continuous running at a comfortable steady pace. Train, don't strain. Start off slowly and gradually increase your distance and pace as you improve and become fitter. To avoid leg injuries, try to run on soft ground and grass – not on the road. Make sure that you invest in a quality pair of running shoes that give comfort and adequate protection against injury.

Cycling can be done out in the fresh air round the roads, or even indoors using an exercise bike. Again, build up slowly and gradually as your level of fitness and endurance increases.

Swimming, too, is an excellent way to build stamina and develop muscular strength, and has the advantage over other forms of exercise that it minimizes the risk of injury when working out in the water.

Skipping can be done literally anywhere at any time and builds stamina plus co-ordination.

Exercises for stamina can be performed in a gym, in your garden, on a football pitch or in your own home. You can plan them as a circuit, ie., a series of exercises performed non-stop or timed with a short rest in between. Here is an example of a stamina-building programme that you can perform in a room at home:

1 Sit-ups
2 Side leg raises
3 Press-ups
4 Bend hops
5 Back raises
6 Twisting
7 Astride (star) jumps
8 Alternate squat thrusts
9 Running on the spot

Each of these exercises should last 30 seconds, with a 30 second rest in between,

building up to three complete circuits.
Power stamina Soccer players who compete at a high level of fitness require power stamina. You can develop this by including some hillwork in your running sessions or by working-out on a treadmill. For example, when running cross-country, run for 30 seconds, rest for 30 seconds building up to 5-10-15 minutes at three-quarters pace. Include some hill running in your training route. Or mark out 50 yards, 100 yards, 200 yards and 400 yards, and run each distance at full speed with a recovery walk back after each.

Stamina-building programme

Sit-ups

1 Lie flat on the floor with knees bent and feet flat on the ground, hands resting on your thighs.

2 Slide your hands up your legs, lifting your torso at the same time. Do 10 repetitions.

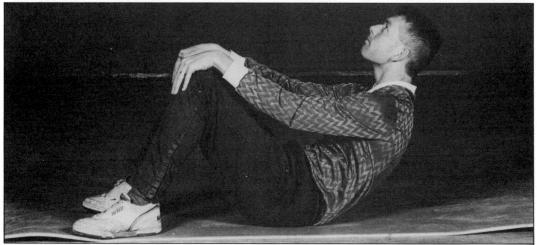

Side leg raises *right*

1 Position yourself on your right side with your weight supported by your right arm and right leg. Keep your shoulder directly above your arm.

2 Raise your left arm and left leg into the air as high as possible and hold. Lower and repeat 10 times each side.

Press-ups *below*

1 Assume the standard press-up position.

2 Do 10 press-ups, keeping your body straight and without your torso touching the ground.

Bend hops

1 Crouch down with your fingertips touching the floor in front of you.
2 Jump straight up, stretching your legs and pointing your toes, keeping your arms straight. Repeat 10 times.

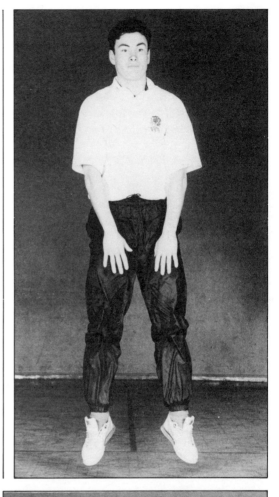

Back raises *below*

1 Lie flat on the ground, hands clasped behind your back.
2 Keeping your legs on the floor, gently raise your torso as far as possible. Repeat 10 times.

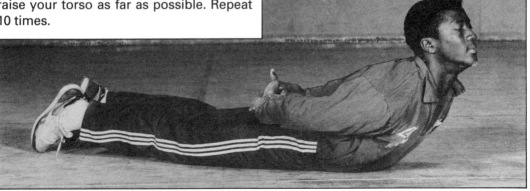

Twisting *below*

1 Stand upright with your feet shoulder-width apart and knees slightly bent.
2 Extend your right arm in front of you and touch your right shoulder with your left hand.
3 Swing your right arm back, twisting your torso. Repeat 10 times on each side.

Astride (star) jumps *below*

1 Stand upright with your arms by your sides.
2 Jump into the air, flinging out both arms and legs as you jump to make the shape of a star. Repeat 10 times.

Alternate squat thrusts

1 Take up a sprint-start position with your shoulders positioned directly above your hands.
2 Now as fast as possible, bring your outstretched leg up to touch your arm with your knee. Keep changing legs. Do 10 repetitions.

Running on the spot

Run on the spot flat-out, lifting your knees as high as possible. Start with 30 seconds, and build up to 1 minute.

More stamina-building exercises

Warm-up relay drill

1 Place two sets of 6 cones 11m/10yd apart in 2 lines.

2 Starting at cone 1, the first player from each team sprints to cone 2 and runs hard on the spot for 10 seconds.

3 He sprints to cone 3 and jogs on the spot for 10 seconds.

4 He sprints to cone 4, and runs flat-out on the spot for 10 seconds.

5 He sprints to cone 5, jogs on the spot for 10 seconds,

6 Then he sprints to cone 6 and runs flat-out on the spot for 10 seconds.

7 He sprints back to the start and the next player from each team takes over.

Walk-jog-sprint

1 Using the perimeter of a football pitch or gym, all players should start at one corner flag.

2 Walk to the next corner flag; then jog along the goal-line to the next corner flag.

3 Then all-out sprint to the half-way line. The sequence is walk-jog-sprint and with every circuit decrease the walking and jogging and increase the sprinting.

4 End with a sprint all around the final circuit.

Pyramid drill

1 All players stand in a line facing a marker 16.5m/15 yd away.

2 All do a press-up, then sprint to the marker and back to the starting line.

3 On reaching the starting line, they jump into the air, at the same time bringing their knees up to the chin.

4 Sprint to the marker and back to the starting line, and do a star jump.

5 Sprint back to the marker, then back to the starting line. **Note:** To do a star jump: jump into the air, throwing your arms and legs out sideways to make the shape of a star. Repeat the whole sequence but doing everything twice except the sprints, which remain constant throughout the exercise. Carry on increasing the sequence by one each time until a maximum of 10 is reached.

Knee squats

1 The players should be divided into two groups and stand facing each other, about 60cm/2ft apart.

2 Both lines should run on the spot.

3 One line stops and stands still and the players extend their arms forwards.

4 The other line tries to touch the outstretched hands with their knees. Continue for 30 seconds, then change and repeat with the other line.

Rotation sprints

1 Place 5 cones in a large circle spaced at random intervals. Divide the team into four groups of equal numbers each standing by a cone, leaving one cone vacant.

2 The team with the vacant cone behind them, should sprint forward to the next one.

3 On reaching that cone the next team then sets off at a sprint towards the next cone. The sequence continues. Besides stamina building this training drill also introduces different running distances and rest periods. This is achieved by leaving different distances between the cones. Uneven rest periods and running distances are an inevitable part of the game of football.

Stamping drill

During the course of a game of football, players will find themselves many times stamping into the ground to either stop or change direction. This stamping uses up valuable energy and should be practised in this stamina-building drill.

1 Place two markers, one at 11m/10yd and the other at 27m/25yd .

2 Players in a line sprint to the 11m/10yd marker, stamp into the ground with one foot and sprint back to the starting line.

3 They then sprint to the 27m/25yd mark and again stamp into the ground, and sprint back to the starting line. Repeat 10 times.

Fireman's sprint *below*

1 Divide into two teams of equal height and weight with no less than five players in each team. Designate a sprinting area of about 22m/20yd or the length of the gym.

2 One player of each team lies on his back and each of his team-mates holds one of his arms or legs.

3 They then carry him to the top of the gym and put him down.

4 All five sprint back to the starting line.

5 A different team-mate lies down and the rest of his team grab his arms and legs and repeat the exercise as below. Repeat until all the players of the team have been carried to the top of the gym. Should there

be more than 5 players in a team, the spare players should follow and sprint back. These spare players must also be carried to the end of the gym before the exercise is completed.

Sprint and dribble drill

1 Divide into two teams of equal numbers, each with a football at one end of the gym. **2** The first player of each team, carrying the ball, sprints to the top of the gym, touches the gym wall, puts the ball down and dribbles it back to his team. Each player in turn repeats the drill. The object is to get the players to dribble at speed. **Note:** The ball must not be kicked ahead.

Tight corner drill *below*

1 This short sprinting exercise is designed to sharpen up speed over 16.5m/15 yd – the average short-sprint distance covered during a match. It also helps players to

change direction faster, which they have to do frequently during a match. As this exercise is performed by individual players, the challenge to improve should be against the clock.

2 Lay out the cones as in the diagram. The first player starts at cone 1.

3 Sprint around the middle cone and touch the top of cone 2 with fingertips.

4 Back around the middle cone and touch cone 1.

5 Then again round the middle cone and touch cone 3.

6 Back around the middle cone and again touch cone 1.

7 Now the long sprint past the middle cone and touch cone 4.

8 Sprint back to cone 1 and finish. It is important that players sprint around the middle cone, and not across it, for this makes them sprint around tight corners which is another aspect of the game covered in this exercise.

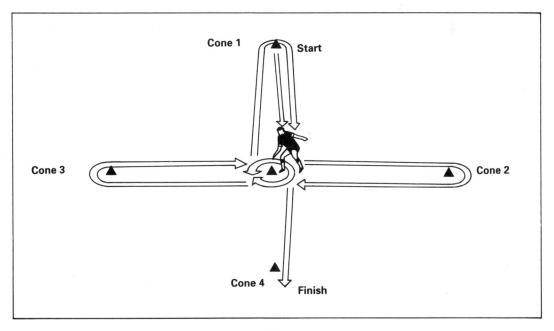

Cone 1   Start

Cone 3   Cone 2

Cone 4   Finish

Running at angle drill *below*

1 Place 3 cones an equal distance apart as shown. Divide once more into two teams of equal numbers.

2 The first player from each team sets off at a sprint – both together. Both touch cone 1, sprint around the top cone on their side and then back to cone 1. The first player to retouch cone 1 is declared the winner. Ensure that the top 2 cones are at an angle to cone 1, for players run at angles on the pitch during a game. The drill is repeated by the whole team.

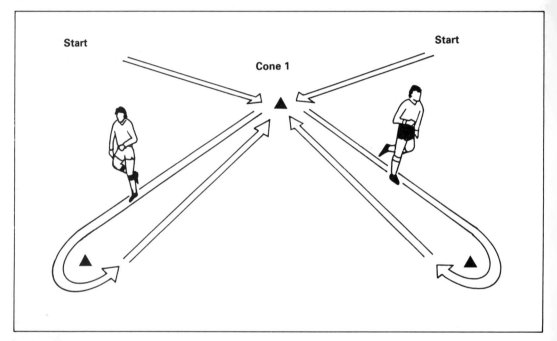

Start

Start

Cone 1

Knee lifts running drill

1 Run gently on the spot for 10 seconds, then, without stopping, run harder, bringing your knees up to shin height for 10 seconds.

2 Back to running on the spot for 10 seconds, and then all-out effort running on the spot raising your knees to knee height for 10 seconds.

3 Continue with gentle running on the spot for 10 seconds, and then accelerate to all-out effort, knees to waist height for 10 seconds.

4 Running on the spot for 10 more seconds, and then harder with knees waist height for 10 seconds.

5 Back to running on the spot for 10 seconds.

6 Bringing knees to chest height, run all-out for the final 10 seconds.

Ground thrust drill

Many times during a game, players may end up on the ground. During this time they are out of the game resulting in their team being short of players. This exercise aims to get players off the ground as quickly as

possible and back into the game.
1 All players sit at one end of the gym facing the wall.
2 On the command they all, in one movement, get up and turn to their right, and sprint to the end of the gym where they sit down and face the wall. Repeat with the players turning to their left when they get up. Repeat 5 times each way.
On every turn alternate between turning left and right to mimic real on-pitch situations during a game when players turn either to their left or right when they get up.

Column drill

1 Form into two or more teams, each in a column.
2 Place a cone 11m/10yd from the front player of each column.
3 The first player from each team sprints around the marker and tags onto the end of his column where he sits cross-legged with arms folded.
4 The rest of the players follow until they have all sprinted and sat down.
5 The first player gets up again and sprints around the marker, tags onto the end of his column, this time lying on his back.
6 The rest of the team follow.
7 When all the players have completed the sprint and are lying down, the first player then takes off and sprints around the marker to return to the end of the column where he lies on his stomach.
8 The rest of the team follow suit.
9 When completed, the first player then makes a final sprint around the marker to join the end of his column. His team-mates follow. The winners are the first team to complete the exercise. This exercise covers several areas; increase in demand; players getting off the ground quickly; competition; and running at angles.

Slalom drill *below*

1 Another sprinting exercise designed to get players to turn left and right quickly. Evenly place six forms in a row. Each team, of an even number of players, has its own row of benches.
2 A player from each team sets off and sprints between the forms and back to the starting line, where a team-mate takes over and follows the same path. Continue until all the players have sprinted. The first team to finish is declared the winners.

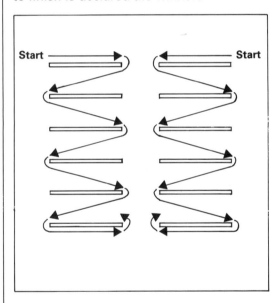

Dribbling drill

1 Set out the teams and forms in the same way as in the previous drill. Each team has a football.
2 A player from each team dribbles the ball between the forms and back to the starting line where a team-mate takes over and repeats. Continue until all the players have completed the exercise. This exercise is designed specifically to get players to dribble the ball with the inside and outside of the foot at speed.

Squat press-ups *below*

1 Assume a press-up position. Bend the left knee between your arms to touch your chin. Keep the right leg straight.

2 Now straighten the left leg and bend your right knee as before. Now bring both legs up between the arms. This exercise should be done slowly at first; increase the pace as your fitness and stamina improve. Do 5 repetitions.

Shuttle runs

1 Set out the cones at 11m/10yd intervals.

2 Divide the players into 2 teams.

3 The first team runs to the top marker and places markers, shirts or bibs on the line of cones.

4 Sprint back to the start.

5 The second team then sprints to pick up the markers and return them to the starting position. Repeat 5 times.

Sprint relay *below*

1 Set out 8 cones as shown.

2 The players should split into two groups and line up behind each of the first cones.

3 A player from each team sets off at a sprint, running from cone to cone and touching each as indicated.

4 He turns at the last cone and repeats the drill in reverse. Encourage players to be the first to touch the middle cone – you don't want losers in your team.

5 As each player finishes, his next team-mate takes over and does the same.

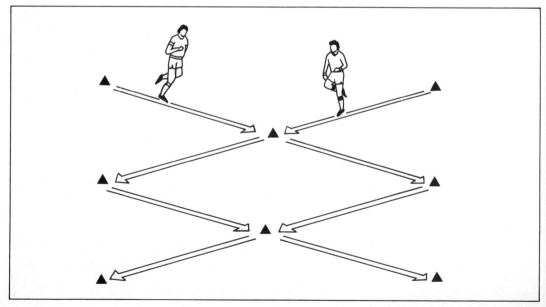

CHAPTER THREE

ABDOMINALS

In the immortal words of an American football coach: 'This man is strong in the mind, but weak in the abdominals'. Abdominal muscles should be firm and strong and, together with the diaphragm, which is situated between the rib cage and the abdominals, they assist breathing when a player is exerted, thus helping the heart and lungs to reduce the oxygen debt more quickly.

Strong abdominal muscles will protect vital organs such as the intestines, solar plexus, colon and stomach. They also link the upper torso with the pelvic girdle. Should the abdominal muscles be slack or, indeed, if the player is overweight in this area, it will hinder him whilst playing because the extra weight will act against gravitational pull resulting in lack of mobility and early breathing stress.

Firm abdominal muscles give a strong downward thrust, creating a firm base for the player. This enables him to keep his feet more firmly on the ground, adding greater balance for change in direction and pace in a match.

You should practise some of the following exercises at home as well as in training sessions, to help build strong muscles and increase flexibility in this area. Remember, however, that it is very important to perfect the techniques involved before increasing the number of repetitions.

Abdominal lifts: 1
1 Lie on your back, hands clasped behind your head, with your legs slightly apart.
2 Push your stomach up into the air with the small of your back off the ground. Keep your head and feet on the ground.
3 Make your body form a 'V' shape. Hold for 5 seconds and then return to the original position. Repeat 10 times. Alternatively, you can turn both knees inwards to touch each other. **Never** do this or any other abdominal exercise with your legs straight.

Bench lifts for legs *below*
1 Sitting on a bench, place your hands flat on the bench about 15cm/6in away from your thighs.
2 Without lifting your body off the bench, stretch both legs straight out in front of you going no higher than hip height. Hold for 10 seconds. Relax and repeat 10 times.

Crucifix drill

1 Lie on your back with both arms outstretched.

2 Bring your right knee up to your stomach, then push the right leg straight into the air.

3 Stretch the right leg over to touch the ground as near to the left shoulder as possible. Repeat with the left leg. Repeat 10 times for each leg.

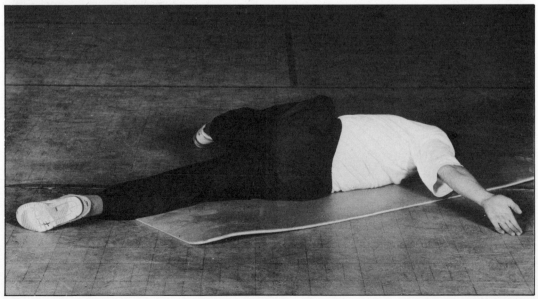

Trunk curls *below*

1 Lie on your back with arms outstretched to the sides, palms flat on the ground. Raise both legs into a vertical position.

2 Keeping both legs together stretch to touch the ground as near to the left shoulder as possible. Repeat on the other side. Repeat 10 times for each shoulder.

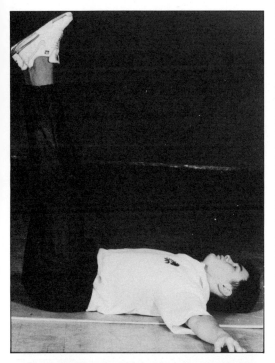

Scissors *above*

1 Lie on your back and raise both arms and legs straight into the air.

2 Keeping your arms up and still, make scissor movements with your legs. Repeat 10 times.

3 Now raise your arms and legs as before but make walking movements in the air with your legs. Repeat 10 times.

Heading the ball drill *above*

1 This exercise is performed in pairs, each with a football. One of the players lies on his back, while the other player, holding the ball, stands about 1.5m/5ft away from his feet.

2 He lobs the ball and the prone player lifts himself up from his trunk only and heads the ball back to his partner. Repeat the exercise 20 times. Change partners.

Pack-backs *opposite*

1 In pairs, with one football, one player lies on his back. The other player, holding the ball, stands about 3m/10ft away from the feet of the prone player.

2 He lobs the ball towards the prone player's feet, who, without raising his body, brings both his knees up and returns the ball to the server by kicking it with the soles of his feet. Repeat 10 times and then change partners.

Half jack-knife *right*

1 Lie on your back and then raise one leg straight into the air.

2 Without moving the raised leg, lift your body up to touch the toes of the raised leg with both hands. Change legs. Repeat 10 times.

Abdominal push

1 Lie on your back with legs together and palms flat on your thighs.

2 Raise your body and, at the same time, slide your hands down the thighs to touch the top of your kneecaps. Do not go any further or your hip muscles will be brought into play. Repeat 10 times.

Leg circles

1 Lie on your back, with legs as wide apart as possible.
2 Raise both legs 15cm/6in off the ground.
3 Without bringing your legs together make small circles with each leg. Continue for 30 seconds without lowering your feet to the ground. Repeat 10 times.

Leg raises

Lie on your back with legs together and raise them both at the same time 15cm/6in off the ground. Hold for 5 seconds. Slowly return your legs to the ground. Repeat 10 times.

Knees and elbows drill

1 Lie on your back, hands clasped behind your head and bring your elbows up around your ears.
2 Lift one knee to touch the opposite elbow, then repeat to the other side. Repeat 10 times for each leg.

Abdominal lifts: 2 *below*

1 Sit on the ground with your legs straight out in front of you and hands clasped behind your head.
2 Without raising your legs, touch alternate kneecaps with your forehead. Repeat 10 times.

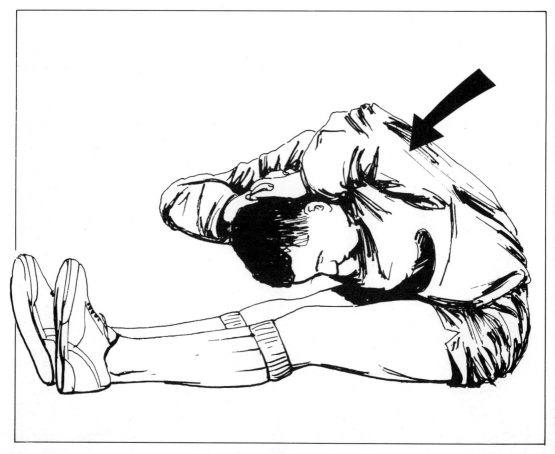

Upper body lift

1 Lie on your back, knees bent and soles of feet firmly on the ground. Stretch out your arms behind your head.

2 Without moving your knees or feet, lift the upper torso off the ground while pushing both hands over your knee caps.

3 Lower your upper body to the ground. Repeat 10 times.

Knee rolls

1 Lie on your back, knees bent and feet flat on the ground, arms fully extended to the sides.

2 Stretching as far as possible and with both knees together, turn to the left and then to the right. Move *only* the knees. Repeat 10 times on each side.

Legs over bench drill

1 Lie on your back with the top of your head facing the side of a bench.

2 With both hands grip the underside of the bench, and bring both legs over and touch the seat of the bench with your toes. Do not release your hands from the bench. Hold for 5 seconds. Return to the original position and repeat 10 times.

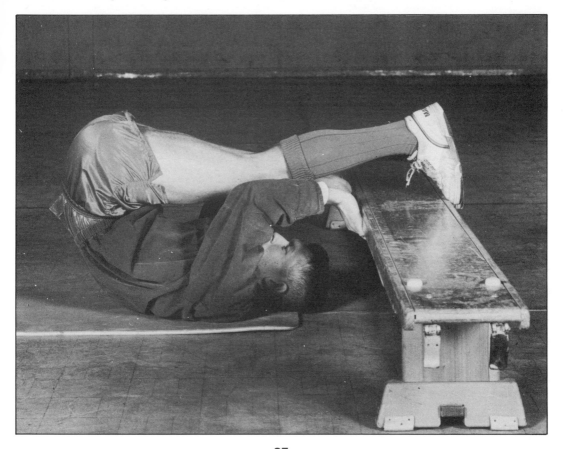

Crossed legs

1 Lie on your back, with legs raised 15cm/ 6in off the ground.
2 Cross your legs over.
3 Then open them as wide as possible.
4 Bring them together again but then cross your legs the opposite way to before. Open them wide and repeat. Hold for 30 seconds each time without lowering your feet to the ground.

Fingers to toes drill *below*

1 Sit up straight with your legs as wide apart as possible.
2 Without bending your knees or bringing your legs together, touch your left toes with your right fingertips while swinging your left arm, as far as possible behind your back. Repeat to the other side and try to obtain a swinging rhythm. Repeat 10 times each side.

Hands to floor *below*

1 Lie down flat on your back with both arms extended fully upwards and knees bent with feet flat on the ground.
2 Raise your trunk and swing your arms, swinging forwards to touch the floor beside your feet. Repeat 10 times.

Body raise

1 Lie on your back, legs straight out together and arms folded on chest.
2 Without unfolding your arms or moving legs, raise your body to a sitting position. Lower and repeat 10 times.

Back stretch drill

1 Lying on your back, bring both knees up to your chin.
2 Then push both legs out sideways and hold for 5 seconds.
3 Bring both legs back together with knees to chin and return to a lying position. Repeat 10 times.

Head to knees drill: 1

1 Lie on your back, knees bent and both feet flat on the ground. Clasp your hands behind your head.
2 Without moving your hands or feet, bring your head up to touch your knees. Repeat 10 times.

Head to knees drill: 2 *below*

1 Lie on your back, hands clasped behind your head and bring both knees up as far as your stomach.
2 Without moving your knees, touch them with your forehead. Return to the original position and repeat 10 times.

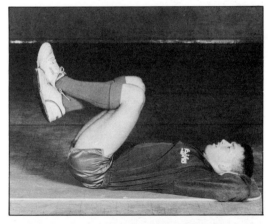

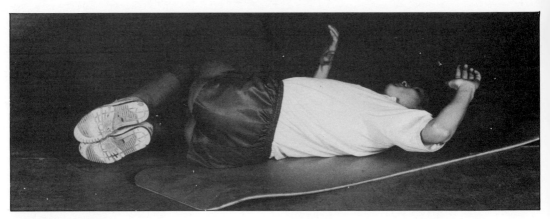

Rolling drill *above*

1 Lie on your back, and bring both knees up to almost touch the stomach, at all times keeping your shoulders on the ground.
2 Roll over to the right so that your right knee touches the ground.
3 Roll back to the centre, and then roll to the left and back to the centre. Repeat 10 times on each side.

Stretching with football *below*

1 Sit up straight with legs wide apart. Using one hand at a time, roll a football in a large circle all the way around your body.
2 Change direction and repeat 5 times each way.

Heels to floor

1 Lie on your back, clasping fingertips behind your neck.
2 Raise your trunk and legs to a vertical position. Lower yourself to the ground. Repeat 10 times.

Raised toe touching

1 Lie on your back, placing both heels on a bench or low wall bar.
2 Without bending your knees, touch your toes with fingertips. Repeat 10 times.

Raised leg relay

Form a circle with all the players sitting down. All raise both legs together into the air and, keeping the legs raised at all times, pass a ball beneath the legs around the circle. Repeat 5 times.

Vertical leg raises

1 Lie on your back, arms at the sides.
2 Keeping both legs straight, raise them to the vertical position. Lower and repeat 10 times.

Bench lifts for arms

1 Lie on a bench with shoulders at the end of the bench and legs supported on the bench or bent with feet on either side.
2 Holding a football, raise your arms above your head then lower to touch the floor. Repeat 5 times.

Hip stretch drill

1 Lie on the ground with arms extended sideways and palms of hands flat on the floor.
2 Raise both legs to a vertical position and, keeping them together, lower them to touch the floor in line with your hips. Raise and repeat 5 times.

Knees to forehead *below*

1 Lying on your back, with both hands grasp your right leg below the kneecap.
2 Keeping the other leg flat on the ground, lift your body and right leg together to touch your right knee with your forehead. Repeat 10 times for each leg.

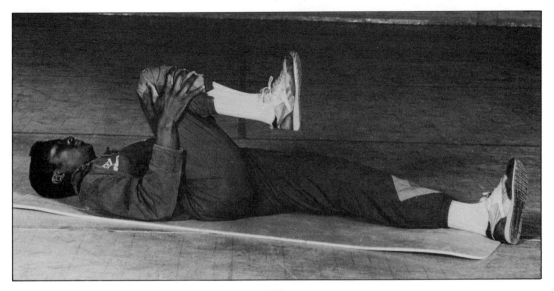

Leg raises with ball *below*

1 Stand with your left foot forward, holding a football on it with your left hand.
2 Keeping your leg straight, raise it as high as possible. Repeat with the right foot. Do 5 repetitions on each side.

High kicks

1 Standing straight, kick your left leg up to touch your right hand held at shoulder height.
2 Repeat to the other side. Do 5 repetitions on each side.

CHAPTER FOUR

ANKLES AND CALF MUSCLES

The ankles and calf muscles are the most important parts of the body in playing soccer. At the apex of the longitudinal arch, a point between the instep and ankle bone, there is an inherent weakness, which can be strengthened by increasing the spring in a powerful ligament that stretches from the calcaneum, front and at the bottom of the ankle bone, to the cuboid, middle of the instep. This is not the only ligament in the ankle for there are many passing in all directions binding the bones together, but it is the most important for our purposes.

Ankles must be kept in a strong flexible condition for they are kicking joints and muscles. During a game of soccer, ankles are under constant strain as players have to turn, kick, tackle and jump. The exercises on the following pages will help not only to strengthen them but also to make them more flexible.

Calf muscles also have to be strong. Their most important function is to hold and support the ankles when you are up on your toes. Whether you are walking, running or jumping, all of them have an on-toes take off. Calf muscles also need to be strong, as do the ankles, for improved turning, kicking, tackling and jumping. Your legs will not tire so easily when the ground gets heavy if you have powerful calf muscles. They also help support the ankles and arches of the foot for increased speed and agility of pace. So you can see why the exercises and drills described here are so important.

Leg extensions: 1 *below*

1 Lie face down on the ground with arms bent below your chin.

2 Keeping your legs straight, raise one leg as high as possible. Repeat 10 times with each leg.

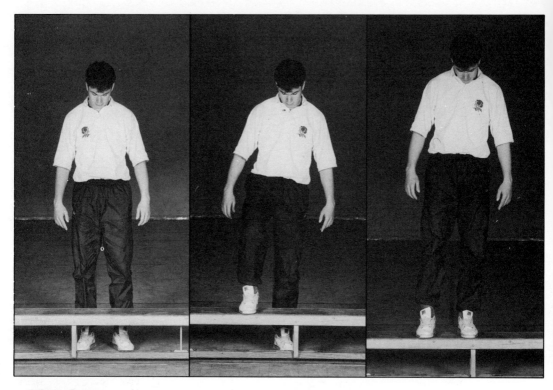

Tackling

Good overall fitness and strength are required for tackling, and special attention must be paid to the legs and upper body. The muscles around the knees and ankle joints have to be strong to take the weight when tackling sideways or head on. The following exercises are particularly good for building fitness for successful tackling:

1 Leg extensions
2 Step-ups
3 Calf raises
4 Hamstring curls
5 Hip and thigh flexing
6 Hill running

Step-ups

1 Stand square to a bench.
2 Step on and off the bench, one foot at a time. Do 10 repetitions. Keep your body straight throughout.

Calf raises

1 Crouch with your feet flat on the floor, your hands resting lightly on your feet, and your head raised.

2 Slowly straighten your legs, raising your body. Lower yourself slowly down to the original starting position. Repeat 10 times.

Hamstring curls

1 Lie face down on the floor with your chin resting on your bent arms.

2 Bend one leg up behind you as far as possible. Repeat 10 times with each leg.

Standing calf stretch: 2

1 Standing, clasp your hands behind your thighs.

2 Slide the clasped hands slowly down your legs as far as possible while bending your trunk forwards. Do not bend the knees. Repeat 10 times.

All-fours calf stretch

1 Standing on all-fours up on tip-toes.

2 Without bending your arms on knees, lower your heels onto the ground. Hold and rise up onto your toes again. Repeat 10 times.

Backwards calf stretch

1 Stand facing a wall and place both hands on it.

2 Without moving your hands walk backwards on your toes as far as possible.

3 Push your heels into the ground. Repeat 10 times.

Standing calf stretch

1 Place both hands on the gym wall, pushing both legs out behind you as far as possible.

2 Keeping your legs straight, rise onto your toes.

3 Lower both heels and press them into the ground. Go back on to tiptoes. Repeat 10 times.

Calf slide and stretch

1 Stand with one foot in front of the other, and, keeping both heels on the ground at all times, slide your feet to increase the distance between them.

2 When maximum stride is achieved, put all your weight on the front foot until you can feel the stretch in the calf muscle of the rear leg. Repeat 10 times each side.

Hip and thigh flexing

1 Stand upright with your hands resting on your hips.

2 Raise one knee in front of you and extend your raised leg. Lower to the ground, and repeat 10 times. Change legs.

Alternate bench stepping

Keeping on your toes throughout this exercise and leading with alternate feet, step on and off a bench. This alternate leading ensures that both ankles are used for pushing off. Repeat 10 times.

Bench jumps

1 Stand astride a bench, up on your toes, and stay up on your toes throughout the whole exercise.
2 Jump to a standing position on top of the bench and immediately jump off to land in the starting position. The astride jump should be performed in a rhythmical manner with no rest on landing. Repeat for one minute.

Ankle hopping

1 One partner lies on the ground while his team-mate stands side-on beside his waist.
2 Keeping his feet together the standing player hops sideways over his partner and straight back again. Repeat 10 times for each leg. Change partners. If no partner is available a football will suffice.

Bench hops

1 Stand side-on to a bench. Standing on the leg nearest to the bench, bend your other leg up behind your back.

2 Hop on to the bench and off the other side. Hopping on and off the bench should be done with alternate legs. Repeat 10 times for each leg.

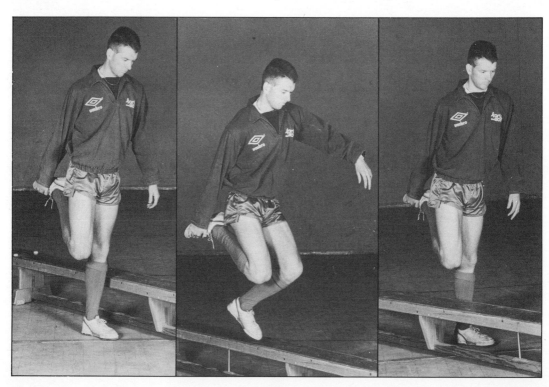

Squat jumps

1 Standing about one foot from a wall and side-on, get into a squat position.
2 Jump up as high as possible and touch the wall with your outstretched arm. Lower yourself down to the squat position. With every jump push up to touch the wall even higher. Repeat 10 times. This exercise is excellent for strengthening ankles and calves.

Kneeling ankle stretch

1 Kneel with both knees pushed into the floor.
2 Sit back on your heels and extend your ankles.
3 Place your hands as far back as possible keeping your knees on the floor. Return to an upright position and repeat 10 times.

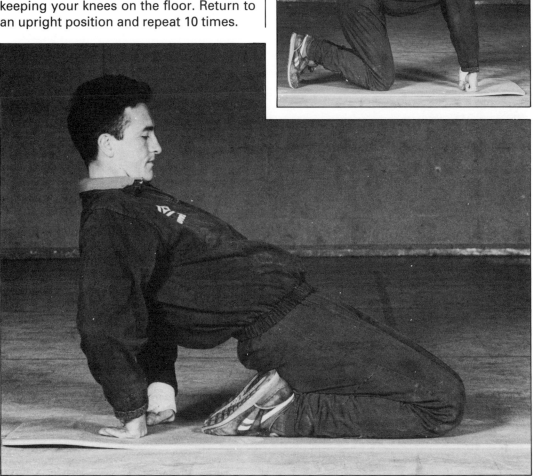

Calf bench stretch
1 Stand on your toes on the edge of a bench and push up fully on your toes.
2 Slowly lower your heels so that they are below the top of the bench. Repeat 20 times.

Ankle stretch
1 Kneel with both hands on the ground level with your shoulders.
2 Push your insteps into the ground, pushing up from the hands only until your knees are off the ground. Keep pushing your insteps into the ground in this way. Repeat 10 times.

Crossed legs stretch
1 Place your left leg in front of your right one, and bend the left knee.
2 Keeping your right leg straight and your heel on the ground, lean forwards to press over the left knee. Stretch slowly and firmly. Repeat 10 times. Change legs.

Skip jumps
1 Starting by standing with legs astride a bench, jump on and off it.
2 Then half turn and jump to face in the opposite direction. Repeat 5 times.

Gym sprints
1 All players gather at one end of the gym. Standing on toes with knees slightly bent about 15cm/6in from the wall, they place their shoulders against the wall behind them.
2 Fully extend both arms out in front shoulder high.
3 On the command, all sprint to the top of the gym, touch the wall and sprint back to the starting line.
4 Take up the original position. The time between the holding position and the sprint is controlled and increased gradually. The standing time starts at 5 seconds, sprint, then 10 seconds, sprint, then 15 seconds, sprint, then 20 seconds, sprint. Increments of 5 seconds are added to the standing time after each sprint ending up with the last standing time of one minute.

Squat stretch
1 Standing on your toes, place your hands on your hips for balance and keep your back straight at all times.
2 Still on your toes, drop down by bending the knees, about 2.5cm/1in and hold for 10 seconds. Continue dropping by 2.5/1in holding for 10 seconds in between until the squat position is reached. Without lowering your heels to the ground, rise gradually from the squat position in the same way, rising by 2.5cm/1in at a time with 10 second intervals until the original standing position is reached.

Thigh squats: 1
1 Standing on your toes, fully extend your arms in front of you at shoulder height.
2 Slowly lower yourself into a squat position and hold for 10 seconds. Return very slowly to the standing-on-toes position. Repeat 10 times.

Heel-walking
Position two cones 20 yards apart. Starting at one cone, walk on your heels to the other cone. Repeat 5 times. This exercise stretches the ankles and calves.

Hill-running
1 Sprint 20-40 yards up a steep slope.
2 Walk down briskly. Repeat 5 times and rest.

CHAPTER FIVE

THIGHS

Quadriceps (the muscles at the front of the thighs) and hamstrings (at the back of the thighs) and the surrounding muscles must be strong to support the knee and hip joints, the latter being the largest joints in the body. This is especially important in soccer when tackling, kicking and changing direction in a big match. Powerful thigh muscles also contribute to good balance. Another advantage of strong thigh muscles is that they may help to prevent cartilage injuries because the thighs are used as shock absorbers.

Cramp is caused by a build up of lactic acid in the muscle due to the cardio-respiratory system's failure to reoxygenate the muscles, and this is most prevalent in soccer during extra time. When cramp occurs in the hamstrings it is usually so debilitating that the player is unable to continue playing. A good balanced training schedule combining drills and exercises for improved speed, stamina, skill and endurance will increase the players' resistance to cramp.

Hip exercise *below*
1 Lie on your side, propped up on one elbow with your top leg crossed over the front of your body and the sole of your foot on the ground.
2 Lift your other leg as far as possible off the ground up and down. At all times, keep the thigh muscles of the lifted leg as tight as possible. Repeat 10 times and change legs.

All-fours thigh stretch

1 Stand on all-fours, arching your back and locking your arms.

2 Without straightening your right leg push it out sideways as far as possible. Return to the original position and repeat with the left leg. Throughout the exercise, do not put your knees on the ground. Do 5 repetitions with each leg.

Side-rolls

1 Sit on the ground with the soles of your feet together.

2 Place your hands on the inside of both knees and roll slowly from side to side. Do 10 repetitions.

Side-holds

1 Lie on your side, and raise your top leg into the air as far as possible.

2 Bring your lower leg up to touch the raised leg. Hold for 5 seconds and return both legs to the ground. Repeat 10 times. Change legs.

Upper body lifts

1 Lie on the ground with arms outstretched to the side level with the shoulders. Keep your knees together and toes pointing outwards.

2 Without moving your legs, push your upper torso into the air. Hold for 5 seconds and then return to the original position. Repeat 10 times.

Quadriceps contraction exercise

1 Sit with your legs out straight in front of you.

2 Tighten and relax the quadriceps (front of the thigh) muscle group. Do 10 repetitions.

Thigh squats: 2

1 Stand about 15cm/6in from a wall and lean back until your back touches the wall.

2 Fully extend both arms out in front of you at shoulder height, and slide back down the wall until you reach a sitting position. Hold for 10 seconds. Return to the original position by sliding up the wall. Repeat 10 times.

Thigh squat on wall

1 Stand with your back about 30cm/12in away from a wall. Bend your right leg up behind you until the heel of your right foot comes into contact with the wall.

2 Keeping your right thigh parallel with the left, raise the heel still further against the wall's solid resistance. Repeat 5 times with each leg.

Hip extension

1 Lie on your side, legs together.

2 Now move the top leg forwards and backwards – do not lift it into the air. Do 10 repetitions and repeat on the other side.

Hamstring stretch: 2

1 Lie face downwards.

2 Raise your left leg off the ground, keeping it straight. Lower and repeat 5 times. Change legs and do 5 more repetitions.

Jack-knife *opposite*

1 Lie on your back and, keeping your legs straight, raise them about 30cm/12in off the floor.

2 Raise your trunk to touch your toes with fingertips. Repeat 5 times.

CHAPTER SIX

LIGAMENTS AND KICKING MUSCLES

Ligaments are the tough fibrous tissue that binds bones together. In layman's terms, ligaments are the strings that make the bones move – like the strings of a puppet.

The kicking muscles cover the ankles, the ligaments behind and around the knees, the hamstrings and groin. It is especially important to stretch the full range of kicking muscles during any warming-up session before training and on match day.

You must stretch the ligaments to get them warm, so that the joints can operate efficiently over the maximum range without damage. For instance, if you are trapping a football while, at the same time, an incoming player catches the inside of the trapping leg, pushing it sideways and backwards, it will result in a stretched groin. This is a serious injury with the possibility of a long lay-off. There are a number of exercises in this chapter that will stretch the groin as far as possible. If they are performed regularly and properly during training, a knock as described above may well not be serious because the groin has already been stretched into that position. Hence the exercises may prevent injury, or, in the event of one, at least reduce the lay-off period.

Exercising the kicking muscles regularly will keep them strong and flexible which will result in greater mobility of players.

Hamstring exercises

Hamstring stretch: 3 *below*

1 Without bending your knees, place one foot in line behind the other as far apart as possible.
2 Very slowly slide both hands down the front of the leading leg as far as possible. Slowly return to the standing position. Repeat 10 times. Change legs.

Caution: At all times, stretching exercises must be done slowly to maximize effect and minimize possible damage.

Head to knee stretch

1 Standing with legs as wide as possible, grasp your hands behind your head.
2 Without bending your knees, slowly bring your forehead down to touch one knee. Hold and then slowly roll up back to the standing position. Repeat with the other knee. Perform 10 times for each leg.

Crossed-leg toe touching

1 Sitting on the ground, fully extend your legs out in front of you.

2 Cross your legs, and keeping them both straight, slowly touch your toes with both hands. After every touch slowly raise yourself to the original sitting position. Repeat 10 times. Change legs.

Stretching in pairs: 1

1 In pairs, sit facing each other, both with your legs fully extended in front of you. Place the soles of your feet against those of your partner and grip each others' hands.

2 Pull your partner forwards as far as possible without raising him from the ground nor forcing him to bend his knees. Repeat 10 times. Change partners and do 10 more repetitions.

Cross-over toe touching

1 Standing upright, cross your legs, with the little toes of each foot touching each other.

2 Without bending your knees, slowly bend forwards and touch your toes with finger-tips. Slowly return to the standing position. Do not raise your heels off the ground. If you are unable to touch your toes, stretch as near as possible to them. Repeat 10 times. Change legs.

Back stretching

1 Standing with your legs as far apart as possible and perfectly straight, touch the ground in front of your feet twice.

2 Touch the ground behind your heels twice.

3 Touch the ground 15cm/6in outside both feet twice.

4 Then bring both arms up as straight as possible above your head, brushing the ears on the way up. Repeat 5 times.

Bending knees-to-head

1 Stand with legs astride, without bending knees, and clasp your hands behind the head.

2 Bend your trunk to waist level and bring one knee up to touch your forehead. Return to the standing position. Repeat 10 times for each knee.

Graded toe-touching

1 Standing with your feet together, without bending your knees touch your toes.

2 Again, without bending your knees, move your feet 15cm/6in apart and touch the outside of each foot with the hand of the same side.

3 Move your feet 30cm/12in apart and again touch the outside of both feet.

4 Stretch your legs as far apart as possible. Do not bend your knees, but touch the outside of each foot. Repeat 5 times.

Leg extension: 2

1 Stand sideways to a wall or wall bars, and hold on to the wall at waist level.

Stand on the leg nearest to the wall, and grasp the toe of the other leg, pulling it forward until it is straight. Lower and pull it up again. Repeat 10 times. Change legs.

Stretching in pairs: 2 *below*

1 In pairs facing each other, you go down on one knee. Your partner fully extends one leg so that his heel is resting on your shoulder.

2 With your partner's heel still on your shoulder, slowly raise yourself until the standing player states that it is far enough. Repeat 10 times. Change legs. Change partners.

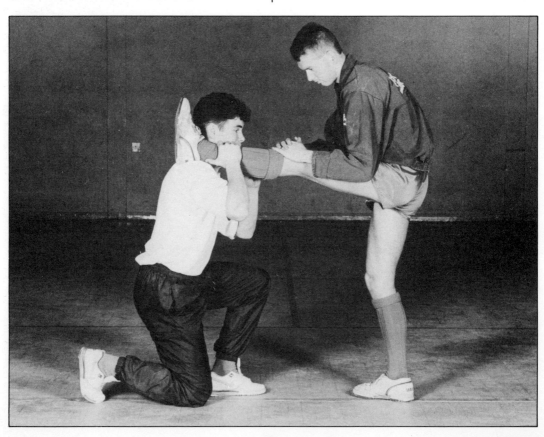

Groin exercises

Groin lunges *right*

1 Stand with your left leg slightly bent forwards and your right leg fully extended outwards and to the side with the sole of the foot on the ground. For balance, place your right hand on your hip.

2 With your left arm extended up and outwards and without moving the sole of the right foot, force your right leg inwards. Keep the leg straight and push your body weight against the right leg. Repeat 10 times. Change legs.

Leg pushing in pairs *below*

1 In pairs, sit facing each other, both with your legs astride.

2 Position your legs inside those of your partner who has his on the outside. Your ankles should touch those of your partner.

3 Now try and push your partner's legs apart. Do 10 pushes and then change legs.

Knee ligament exercises

One-legged stretch

1 Stand on your left leg and bend your right leg up behind you, grasping your foot in your right hand.

2 With slow, firm stretches, pull your right foot up as far as possible. To aid balance, extend your free arm up and outwards. Repeat 10 times. Change legs.

Piggy-back drill

1 In pairs of equal height and weight, take up a 'piggy back' position on your partner's back.

2 He slowly lowers himself into a sitting position, but not any further because excess strain will be put upon his knee ligaments. He slowly returns to the standing position. During all this time you must not move, or serious strain will be put on your partner's knees. Repeat 10 times. Change partners and let him climb on your back.

CHAPTER SEVEN

LEGS

Legs are the hallmark of the type of activity a sportsman performs. For example, a distance runner has very slim but elongated, enduring calf muscles allowing for good long strides over distance. Whereas, at the other extreme, a downhill skier requires slim almost non-existent calves but very powerful thigh muscles to hold dynamic squat positions in order to absorb the vibration of the ground and maintain good balance over short periods. However, the footballer needs a combination of both.

Strong upper and lower leg muscles are required for jumping. As the lower legs and feet are the furthermost parts of the body from the heart, they need a fit and efficient circulatory system to supply oxygenated blood quickly to offset fatigue and avoid over-use injuries.

To achieve this, a foundation of aerobics (the ability of the heart and lungs to provide oxygenated blood to the muscles during prolonged activity) must be acquired in pre-season training and then maintained throughout the season in order to complement anaerobic capacity (the ability to repay back incurred oxygen debt quickly after the short dynamic activity-type training of a footballer).

Sitting groin stretch

1 Sit on the floor, the soles of the feet together and holding both feet with your hands.
2 Place your elbows on the inside of your knees and lean over to touch your toes with your forehead. Repeat 10 times.

Squat thrusts

1 Adopt a crouching position, up on your toes.
2 Stretching as far forward as possible, put your fingertips on the floor, and, without moving them, straighten your legs to a standing position. Repeat 5 times.

Bouncing squats

1 Squat down on your toes. To gain balance, place your hands on hips or one hand on a wall.
2 Bounce up and down to about waist height. Repeat 10 times.

Raised hamstring stretch

1 Place one heel at hip height on a wall bar.
2 Keeping both legs straight, touch the toes of your raised leg with your fingertips. Repeat 10 times on each leg.

Sideways calf stretch

1 Stand facing a wall with both hands placed on the wall.
2 Bend your supporting leg until you reach a squat position.
3 Kick out sideways and point the toes of the non-standing leg. Raise yourself up again. Repeat 10 times. Change legs.

Standing knee to forehead

1 Standing on one leg, bring the other one up to your waist.
2 Lower your forehead to touch the raised knee. Hold for 5 seconds. Repeat 10 times. Change legs.

Stand-up jack-knife *below*

1 Jump into the air bringing your legs out straight in front of you and forwards.
2 Touch your toes. Do 5 repetitions.

Skip jumping

At a given count, jump into the air opening and closing your legs. Repeat the exercise 10 times.

Hop and walk circuit

1 Mark out an area 11m/10yd square with a numbered cone at each corner. Starting at cone 1, walk to the third cone.
2 Hop on your right leg to the fourth cone.
3 Walk to the second cone.
4 Hop on your right leg to the fourth cone.
5 Walk to the first cone.
6 Hop to the fourth cone. Without stopping, repeat the sequence using the left leg. Finish by 'bunny-hopping' around all four cones.

Thigh squats

1 Stand with hands on hips.
2 Raise your heels and bend your knees. Repeat 10 times.

Resistance in pairs

1 In pairs sitting with legs apart opposite each other, place one leg on top of your partner's leg who then does the same with his other leg.
2 Both try to lift each other's partner's leg against resistance.

Squats with ball

1 Standing with both arms fully extended at chest level, hold a football in the up-turned palms of your hands.
2 Keeping your arms outstretched, bend to a squat position. Rise and repeat 5 times.

Bunny hops: 1

Place 2 markers 22m/20yd apart and, starting at one marker, with feet together hop to the next marker. Repeat 5 times. Change legs. As a variation, try hopping, stepping and jumping; or stepping followed by a two-footed jump.

Bunny hops: 2

1 Standing on your toes, fully extend your arms out in front of you at shoulder height.
2 Without putting your heels on the ground do 'bunny hops' between the markers, set at 22m/20yd intervals.

Bunny hops: 3

1 Standing on your left leg, hold your right foot in your right hand bent back behind you.
2 Hop on one foot to a marker 22m/20yd away. Repeat with the other foot.

Piggy-backs

1 Place 2 cones 22m/20yd apart and divide into pairs of equal height and weight.
2 One player gives his partner a 'piggy-back' and carries him between the cones. Change partners.

One-legged squats

1 Stand on one leg and bend the other back behind you. Extend both arms out sideways at shoulder level.
2 Slowly bend the standing leg into a squat position. Return slowly to the standing position. Throughout this exercise do not lower your arms nor the non-standing leg. Repeat 10 times. Change legs.

Hop and stretch drill: 1

1 Stand with hands on hips.
2 Hop on one leg with the other leg swinging sideways. Repeat 10 times on each leg.

Hop and stretch drill: 2 *above*

1 Standing with hands on hips, hop on the spot.
2 At the same time, raise the opposite knee to waist height. Repeat 10 times on each leg.

Russian dance

1 Squat with knees fully bent and hands on hips.
2 Do a Russian dance step with the forward heel touching the ground. Repeat with the other leg.

Seated ball kicks

1 In a sitting position, rest a ball on your feet.
2 Raise your legs, keeping them straight to kick the ball into your hands. Repeat 5 times.

Forward jumps

1 Standing with feet together, jump forwards.
2 Jump into the air with knees fully bent. Repeat the sequence until you reach a marker positioned 22m/20yd away.

Goalkeeper jumps

1 Pushing off with either foot, jump to save an imaginary football, as a goalkeeper would do.
2 With arms fully extended above head, jump sideways. Repeat on the other leg to the other side 10 times.

Fireman's lift

1 In pairs, pick up your partner using a 'Fireman's Lift'.
2 Slowly bend your knees until they are half bent, then straighten them until you are standing upright again. Repeat 5 times. Change partners.

CHAPTER EIGHT

DORSAL MUSCLES

Dorsal muscles are back muscles. They are situated on either side of the back bone, and, if strong, they will help prevent slipped discs. Toned-up dorsals will make a player more flexible when twisting and turning during a game, a common occurrence in a game of football.

These muscles also need to be strong to take the buffeting encountered in collisions with other players during a match. When a player falls to the ground landing on his back, the toned-up back muscles will absorb the impact thereby enabling the player to get back into the match more quickly.

The set of exercises outlined in this chapter are designed mainly for the dorsals but are equally useful for strengthening the torso and shoulder muscles, which are also used in twisting and turning and maintaining balance. A useful side-effect of strengthening dorsals is that they will help ward off back strain during everyday life.

Upper body strength is important in order for a player to stay on his feet during a tackle and to keep possession of the ball.

Upper body circles

1 Stand with legs astride and the hands clasped behind the head.
2 Without bending your knees and keeping both feet on the ground, use the whole of the upper body to make deep circles. Do 5 repetitions each way.

Standing back stretch

1 Stand up straight.
2 Bend backwards with your arms raised forwards and upwards. Repeat 5 times.

Front raise *below*

1 Lie on your stomach, clasping both hands on your buttocks.
2 Lift both legs and your head at the same time. Lower and repeat 5 times.

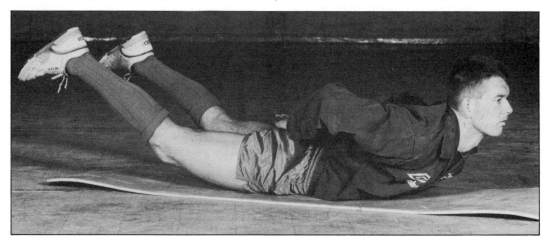

Ankle curls

1 Lie flat on your back and lift up both knees to waist height and grasp your ankles.
2 Without losing this grip, lift your head to touch your knees. Repeat 5 times.

Buttock raise

1 Take up a squat position with both feet on the ground and both hands stretched out in front with palms flat on the ground.
2 Without moving your hands, raise your buttocks as slowly as possible. Do 5 repetitions.

Half jack-knifes

1 In a sitting position, bring up both knees keeping your feet on the ground.
2 Place your hands under your thighs and lower your forehead to the knees. Now rock to and fro. Repeat 5 times.

Hand sliding drill

1 In a standing position, slide your hands down the side of each leg, reaching as far as possible without bending forwards.
2 When this position is reached, hold for a count of 4. Repeat 10 times.

Trunk twists

1 Stand with legs astride and fully extend both arms above your head.
2 Bend forwards from the trunk until your body is in an 'L' shape.

3 Without bending the arms or knees, slowly twist as far as possible the top half of the body first to the left and then to the right. Repeat 5 times each side.

Calf stretch with wall

1 Stand facing a wall, with the palms of both hands flat on the wall. Walk backwards as far as possible until fully stretched and on your toes.
2 Lift one leg up as far back as possible. Repeat 10 times for each leg.

Back arching

1 Stand with hands clasped behind your back.
2 Lean forward and, without breaking your grasp, pull both arms to the side of your head. Do 5 repetitions.

Knees to shoulders

1 Sit on the ground with both arms fully extended forwards.
2 Bring your left knee up to touch your left hand. Repeat on the other side. Do 5 repetitions on each side.

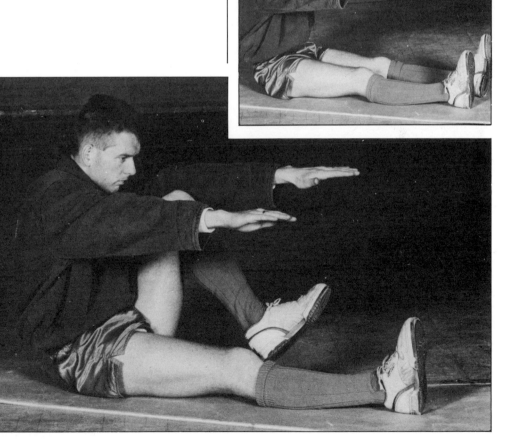

Press-ups with ball *above*

1 Lie on top of a football in a press-up position with only your toes touching the ground, and both arms fully outstretched sideways.

2 Look up at the sky and hold this position for 10 seconds. Relax. Repeat 5 times.

Back jack-knifes

1 Lie on your stomach with arms fully extended in front of you.

2 Lift your arms, raise your head backwards, and bend your knees to bring your legs up over your back. Hold for a count of 4. Repeat 5 times.

CHAPTER NINE

UPPER TORSO

The heart is a muscle, just like the biceps or the calf, and to exercise the heart and lungs, we have to increase the oxygen requirements of the body. This can be achieved by aerobic exercise, such as running or jogging. How hard the heart muscle is exercising can be measured by taking a reading of the pulse rate. The speed at which the heart beats depends on the oxygen content of the blood and, if the oxygen level falls, the heart beats faster. Therefore if you exercise the large muscle groups in the trunk, arms and legs, which use up a great deal of oxygen, your pulse rate will rise.

To take your pulse, turn the palm of the hand upwards with the wrist bared. Lightly place the first three fingers of the left hand just above the heel of the right thumb. Count off the beats for 6 seconds, then multiply by 10 to give the rate per minute. To obtain the pulse rate subtract your age from 200, and then subtract the unfitness handicap of 40 (lower to say 20 when fitter), and the final figure is your own personal pulse rate.

In normal quiet respiration, only a fraction of the total lung volume is used. The total amount of air that can be inhaled into the lungs is called 'vital capacity'. During training the vital capacity is improved, but it must be borne in mind that a player's size bears some relation to his individual vital capacity.

Shoulders need to be strong for balance when sprinting and running. When running the body is off-centre of balance, and the cadence of the arm movement will reflect this. With the amount of arm movement made during a game of football, weak shoulders will ensure that players will tire more quickly. Strong shoulders are also needed for absorbing and withstanding collisions with other players and the ground during a match.

Shoulder rolling

1 Stand with your arms out in front at shoulder level and hands facing upwards.
2 Make 10 large circles one way and then 10 large circles the opposite way.
3 Clap your hands high above your head, then lower them to clap hands behind thighs. Do not bend your knees. Repeat 10 times.

Opposite stretching

1 Stand with your feet slightly apart and palms of your hands on your thighs.
2 Without leaning forwards or bending your knees, push your right hand down the side of your right leg. Bring your left hand up to the left armpit. Return to the upright position. Repeat 10 times. Change arms.

Aeroplane rotation

1 Stand with your legs slightly astride, both arms out sideways at shoulder level.
2 Rotate both arms simultaneously to make small circles.
3 Gradually make larger circles until you are making circles by using the whole circumference of both arms.
4 When this point is reached, stop, and hold both arms out sideways at shoulder level.

5 Without dropping your arms, bend them and push them both out to full extension 3 times.

6 Again, without dropping your arms, make large circles in the opposite direction, gradually reducing them to make minute circles.

Press-ups and headers

1 In pairs: stand facing each other about 5.5m/5yd apart. One player has a football.

2 The player with the ball serves it to his partner who heads the ball back to the server and then immediately does a press-up. Return to the standing position. Repeat 10 times. Change servers.

Back resistance *below*

1 In pairs: sit back-to-back with elbows linked.

2 One player tries to get up while the other tries to hold him down. Take it in turns. Repeat 10 times.

Back rotation

1 Stand with legs astride, arms forward at shoulder level.

2 Turn your head, arms and shoulders around to the left as far as possible.

3 Bend your right arm across your chest. Repeat this movement to the right. Throughout the exercise keep your hips and legs still. Do 5 repetitions on each side.

Resistance with wall

1 Stand facing a wall, placing one foot in front of the other for stability.

2 Rest the palms of your hands on the wall and push as hard as possible against the wall. Repeat 10 times. Change legs.

Back straightener with partner

1 In pairs, stand back to back with inter-locked arms.

2 One player bends forwards and lifts his partner onto his back.

3 Without breaking the arm lock, the carried player slides off his partner and straight away lifts him onto his back. Repeat 10 times.

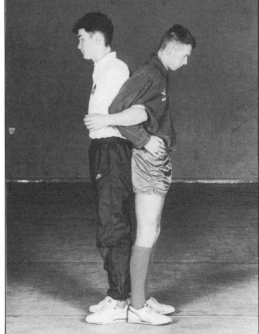

CHAPTER TEN

GENERAL EXERCISES

After achieving all-round fitness and strength, some footballers need to improve their heading and shooting skills by exercises to develop specific muscle groups.

Heading
This requires strong neck muscles and powerful legs along with good technique and timing. Light weights can be used in the gym to build up muscles around the neck. Some good exercises are:

1 Upright rowing

2 Lateral raises

3 Pushing your neck against resistance, eg. your hand

Leg power can be achieved by step-ups, squat-hopping and bounding, and using weights if required.

Some good practice drills for heading the ball are as follows:

1 Head a ball fed from a player at 5, 10, 15 and 20 yards away.

2 Head the ball to return the goalkeeper's kick-outs.

3 Bound up stairs or terraces on one leg, and then with double hops.

Caution: It is a known medical fact that a fully fit athlete can sustain all-out effort for only 45 seconds. This should be borne in mind when performing pressure-training exercises. The exercise should cease at 45 seconds or when technique fails, which ever comes first.

---

4 Do standing jumps, followed by squat jumps.

A strong back is very beneficial in heading and can be achieved by performing exercises regularly for the stomach and back, either at home or in the gym. For example:

Stomach: 1 Sit-ups (bent leg)

2 Bent leg raises

Back: 1 Prone leg raises

2 Back arching

Shooting
The principal fitness qualities required for shooting are flexibility, leg strength and good balance. The actual striking of the ball with the foot works the kicking muscles, and a series of repetitions and practising your shooting will increase your leg power.

The following exercises will also prove helpful:

1 Circle jumping

2 Trunk rotations

3 Twisting

4 Working out with weights to strengthen your hips and thighs.

To improve your balance you can try walking along a beam, skipping, astride jumps and sideways running.

General exercises

Kangaroo jumps
1 From a standing position, lower yourself down to a squat position.

2 Kick out your legs behind.

3 Do a press-up.

4 Bring your legs back to a squat position.
5 Return to a standing position. Repeat 20 times.

Touch the marker drill

1 In pairs: one player stands between markers 9m/8yd apart. His partner, facing him, also stands between markers but these are 6.5m/6yd apart.
2 The player standing between the 9m/8yd markers is the attacker, and his opponent is the defender. The attacker tries to touch one of his own markers before the defender can touch his own. The attacker tries to dummy his opponent. The time allowed for this exercise is one minute.

Speed test

1 For speed and agility on foot: set up cones in a 22m/20yd square. Place a further cone in the middle of the square.
2 A player stands by each outside cone.
3 All 4 players set off at the same time and all try to be first to touch the middle cone and then return to the top cone of their alley.

Piggy-back endurance

1 In pairs of equal height and weight, take up piggy-back positions.
2 Have a one-lap race. Change partners at the end of the lap.

Body swerving drill

1 Set out 4 cones 11m/10yd square with 2 players in the square. One is an attacker and the other a defender.
2 To score a goal, the attacker must touch a cone with his hand. Should he touch a cone behind the defender he scores 2 goals. The defender tries to cut off the attacker's path. The main aim of this set-up is to get attack-ers moving and wrong-footing defenders. However, it can also be used for short sprints, twisting and turning – all of which happen during a game. Change after 10 attempts at goal.

Standing jumps *below*

1 Stand with feet together and knees slightly bent.
2 Jump into the air, at the same time bringing your knees up to the chest. Repeat 10 times.

Heading game

1 Set up 2 corner flags as goals. The distance between the flags will vary according to how many players are involved.

2 Divide into teams of equal numbers.

3 To score a goal, throw the ball to your partner who has to head the ball against the corner flag. Players are not allowed to throw the ball to themselves. Players move from side to side. This helps strengthen the neck muscles. In matchplay terms it enhances the need for players to recognise the need to support the player with the ball; and also the value of running into a space.

Heading in a circle

1 Players form a circle, each holding a football. One player stands in the centre of the circle.

2 The player in the centre faces an outer player who lobs the ball at him. He heads the ball back to him and then faces another player. This will get the heading player to jump, twist and turn and quicken his reactions.

Goalkeeping exercise: 1

1 With 2 cones make a goal.

2 The player with a football stands 10 or 20 yards from the goal, and then kicks the ball with a pushing action so as to make the goalkeeper save.

Goalkeeping exercise: 2

1 Set up as in the previous exercise. The goalkeeper stands with his back to the player with the ball.

2 The player with the ball calls that he is about to kick the ball, and at the same time the goalkeeper turns around to save the ball.

Goalkeeping exercise: 3

1 Make a goal with 2 cones. The players form into 2 lines; line 1 stands in front of the goal, and the other line behind it.

2 Each player in line 1 has a football. Each, in turn, throws the ball at the goal for the goalkeeper to save.

3 When saved, the goalkeeper then passes the ball to the line behind the goal. Should he fail to save the ball it is fielded and retained by the line behind the goal. When all the footballs are in the possession of the players behind the goal, the goalkeeper turns round and the procedure is repeated.

Up off the ground exercise

1 Lie on your back with arms outstretched above your head holding a football with both hands.

2 Throw the ball into the air.

3 Get up and catch the ball before it touches the ground. Return to the original lying-down position. Repeat 10 times.

One-to-five exercise

This exercise consists of 5 parts. All players jog around the perimeter of the gym or playing area. On command they shall:

1 Raise their right arms aloft.

2 Raise their left arms aloft.

3 Touch the ground with their right hands.

4 Touch the ground with their left hands.

5 Touch the ground with both hands at the same time.

Players must not lower their arms nor raise their hands until ordered to do so. All movements must be carried out whilst jogging. Should any player get out of sequence he does 5 press-ups. This exercise is designed for promoting endurance and concentration.

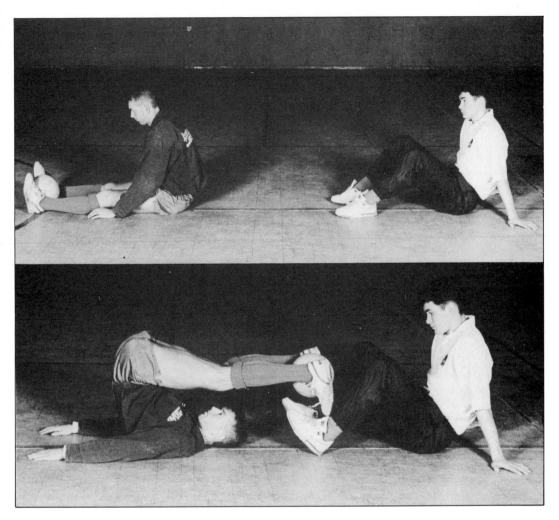

Bench race drill

1 At even intervals, place some benches in a row.

2 Start at one end and sprint and jump over the benches.

3 Touch the wall at the other end and return to the start by sprinting and jumping over the benches. This can be turned into a competition exercise by having 2 or more teams.

Backwards passing drill *above*

1 Players lie down in rows behind each other.

2 The first player of each row has a football between his feet.

3 Rolling over yourself, backwards pass the ball with your feet over your head to your next team-mate.

4 He grasps the ball with his feet and passes it on. Continue until all the players in each row have passed the ball on.

Ground leap-frog

1 In two teams of equal numbers: the first player goes down on the ground in a crouched position and sideways to his team.

2 The next player jumps over the crouched player and then takes up the same position some 5.5m/5yd away. This continues until all the members of the team are lined up in the crouched position.

Sprint circuits

1 Place some benches firmly against the wall of the gym so that they will not slip.

2 Players gather at the other end of the gym and all sprint to the benches and, using both feet at the same time, hop on and off the bench 10 times.

3 They sprint back to the other end of the gym. Repeat 10 times.

Throwing relay

1 The players in each team stand behind each other in a line facing the leader, who throws the ball to the first man in the line.

2 He returns it and kneels down.

3 The leader throws the ball to the second player who returns it and kneels down, and so on through the team.

4 When the ball reaches the last player, instead of returning it, he takes the place of the leader, who takes the place of the first player, and the whole line moves down one place. This is repeated until each player has had his turn at being the leader.

Football tennis

The server may either kick or head the ball over the net; the receiver may return by kicking or heading. The ball may bounce once only on each side of the net before returning. Each side serves the ball 5 times before the service changes. The first team to score 15 points wins.

Agility circuit

1 Place 6 cones in a line at 11m/10yd intervals.

2 The first player then sprints to the first marker.

3 Do a star jump.

4 Sprint to the second marker.

5 Sprint to the third marker.

6 Do a sit-up.

7 Sprint to the fourth marker.

8 Do one burpee.

9 Sprint to the fifth marker.

10 Now all-out running on the spot for 10 seconds.

11 Sprint to the sixth marker.

12 Jump to head an imaginary football.

13 All-out sprint back to the starting line.

This exercise can be turned into a competition with relay teams.

Indian file

The players jog around the pitch in file formation. The last man chooses his moment to sprint along the outside of the file to take up the front position. The pace of the jog is set by the leading man. The end man sprints to the front to take over the lead in a continuous process.

Chipping exercise

1 The players, each with a ball, run around the perimeter of the playing area.

2 On reaching a marker, each in turn makes a lofted pass to the goalkeeper, G1, and then sprints ahead to receive the return throw from the goalkeeper. At the other end, the players repeat the same exercise using goalkeeper G2.

Hip exercise with wall

1 Stand facing the wall and place both hands on the wall.

2 Push your right leg out sideways. Then draw it across the front of the body out to the left. Obtain a swinging motion. Repeat 10 times. Change legs.

Leg swings

1 Stand sideways to a wall.

2 Swing your outside leg first backwards, then forwards, to the middle and stop.

3 Push the leg out sideways, then lift it up and down twice. Repeat 10 times. Change legs and repeat 10 times.

Combining practice matches with exercises

Most training sessions end with a practice match so that basic skills may be practised. If the match is at the end of the session, players tend to look towards the end, but I feel that a better way is to combine training with the match by playing a match throughout the whole of the session. When the ball goes out of play or a foul is committed, stop play and do a series of exercises. Then restart the match. Do not stop play when a player shoots or heads at goal, and the ball goes out of play or he scores. This will not encourage players to shoot at goal because if they miss they will have to do exercises. This fear of shooting may well spill over to match day. If players do not shoot they will not score, and shooting must be encouraged at all times. This match exercise syndrome will be more interesting for the players and indeed for their coach too.

Cycling *below*

1 Lie on your back and push both legs into the air. Support your body by placing both hands under your buttocks.

2 Make a cycling motion in the air with your legs.

3 Release your hands and lower the legs to 15cm/6in above the ground.

4 Make a pedaling motion with both legs. Without letting the legs touch the ground, go back to the cycling position. Repeat each part 5 times.

EQUIPMENT AND INJURIES

The right equipment

When selecting new football boots or trainers, it is advisable to ensure that there is adequate protection around the toes, heels and instep. However, the most important thing to look for is that the sole of the foot is fully covered by the sole of the boot so that none of the foot is hanging over the sole of the boot. A snug-fitting boot will ensure that no rubbing of the toes, sides of the feet or heels takes place whilst running.

Ill-fitting boots will lead to blisters and legs tiring very quickly during a game, as they will cause you to run with an awkward stance to relieve the discomfort of the feet.

Football boots or trainers should not be laced in a criss-cross manner, but looped. Should you receive any injury whereby the boot has to be removed, it is very easy to run a pair of scissors down the instep through the looped lace to cut them because you need only cut one lace, making it easy to prise open the boot for removal and, at the same time, causing the least discomfort to the player. With criss-crossed lacing, scissors cannot be simply run down the instep but instead every single lacing on both sides of the boot will have to be cut before the boot can be removed, causing extra distress to the player and may even result in causing additional damage to the injury.

What to do with injuries

Should a player sustain a twist, damage to a muscle or ligaments he should be removed from the field immediately. The following procedure should be followed: it is easy to follow by remembering the word 'RICE' (Rest, Ice, Compression, Elevation).

Rest is the best way to avoid further damage. Do not exercise even after a minor tear because of the chance of increasing the initial degree of bleeding.

Ice should be applied to the site of the injury as soon as possible and should last for a period of 15-20 minutes. Ice should not be applied direct to the skin for fear of adding ice burns. Cooling is a good analgesic. If ice is not available, running cold water will suffice.

Compression: the injured part must be immobilized for the next 36-48 hours. Over-enthusiastic tight bandaging is counter-productive. Prolonged compression is equally pointless.

Elevation drains the bruise upwards instead of downwards. Elevation is essentially an early measure designed to mini-mize initial damage.

Index